Old Man
of
The Mountains

Old Man
of
The Mountains

The Story of Peter Voiss, California's Most Notorious, Eccentric
Gold Prospector
Of the 20th Century

Brookelea Heintz Lutton

Gold Dust Publishing

July 2008

To the memory of George Albert Heintz
1906-1988

Old Man of the Mountains
The Story of Peter Voiss, California's Most
Notorious, Eccentric Gold Prospector of the
20th Century

Published by Gold Dust Publishing
P.O. Box 582424
Elk Grove, CA 95758
Email: golddustbooks@surewest.net
Website: www.golddustpublishing.com

Cover design and interior layout by Mustang Graphic
Designers, MustangGraphic@aol.com

ISBN: 978-0-9815913-0-8

"And he that sat upon the throne said, Behold, I make all things new. And he said unto me, Write: for these words are true and faithful."

Rev. 21:5

Table of Contents

Acknowledgments...................................... ix

Introduction... xi

Chapter 1   The Pencil................................ 1

Chapter 2   The "Find"................................. 3

Chapter 3   The Early Years........................... 15

Chapter 4   Mining Years.............................. 19
             My Burros or Donkeys! by Peter Voiss....... 23

Chapter 5   The Roaring Twenties.................. .33
             The Prospector by Peter Voiss................ 34

Chapter 6   Depression Years........................ 37

Chapter 7   Stop, or I'll Shoot!....................... 41

Chapter 8   The Trial.................................. 49

Chapter 9   After the Trial............................ 61
             Letter from a Friend......................... 64

Chapter 10   Return to Freedom...................... 67
             Animal Life and Their Reason Power 68
             by Peter Voiss
             Ivory Soap by Peter Voiss....................... 72

Chapter 11   The Accident................................ 75
              Promise to Donkeys After the Accident 76
              by Peter Voiss

Chapter 12   Mad as a Hatter........................... 79

Chapter 13   Women and the Road.................... 81
              The Unsuccessful Buggy Ride by Peter
              Voiss..81
              The Dream Baby by Peter Voiss................ 83

Chapter 14   New Baby and the Fair.................. 85

Chapter 15   War Years................................... 95

Chapter 16   End of the Trail............................ 99
              Sadly I Leave You by Peter Voiss........... ..102

Chapter 17   On Reflection.............................. 103

Acknowledgments

Thank you to the following:

Ralph Pearce of the Dr. Martin Luther King, Jr. Library, California Room, San Jose, for assisting me with the old newspapers.

The staff of the Dr. Martin Luther King, Jr. Library, San Jose, for their patience and courtesy.

The staff of the California State Library, California Room, sacramento, for their patience and courtesy during my many visits.

Diane Borden, my good friend and confidante, for her input and support of this project during our Saturday morning walks.

Howard "Butch" Stitt, retired teacher, Del Oro High School, Loomis, CA, for his input.

Gary Noy, author and history teacher at Sierra College, Rocklin, CA, for his suggestions.

My editor, Teresa Coates, for her expertise of the English language. I am truly grateful for her ability to "draw me out" in order to clarify and expand on my writing.

My husband Ron for his love and support during yet another of my ventures.

A very special thanks to my "big" sister Barbara Seevers for encouraging me to finish the project our father started so long ago.

Introduction

For nearly sixty years a piece of California's history has been in my family's possession. My father found a black purse in a mineshaft that contained the last personal effects of an old gold prospector, Peter Voiss. He didn't know what to do with the belongings. He toyed with the idea of finding out more about him and writing his story, but he really didn't have the tools or know-how to do the research. In the 1950s he had a buyer for the purse and its contents, but he didn't know its worth, so he didn't follow through and the purse just sat in a drawer gathering dust. He did start to write the story, but like many other aspects of my father's life, he didn't get beyond the first couple of paragraphs.

After my father's passing in 1988, I came into possession of the purse. I dug it out a few times over the years, looked at its contents and muddled over what to do with it myself beyond the research I had begun in 1987. As the years progressed and thoughts of the purse kept popping into my head, my choices seemed to be centered on either selling it to a collector or donating it to a historical society or archives. But then the prospector's story wouldn't be told.

Peter Voiss had written stories about his life living in the mountains with his burros. These stories were in the purse. His stories take you deep into the mountains and gulches of the Sierra Nevada and on the roads throughout California's Mother Lode as he traveled with his burros in his makeshift cart. He describes his love affair with his burros, his best friends. His written descriptions are as he spoke, in a combination of broken English and German. I have included his stories as he wrote them.

One recent day I made the decision and commitment to follow through on what my father was unable to do. I sat down at the computer and started to write; I decided that Peter Voiss' story would be told. A piece of California's Gold Country history would be preserved. It is about an honest-to-goodness gold prospector wandering California's highways and byways with his cart and burros, and what it was like living a solitary life in the mountains and outskirts of Bay Area cities. It is about his scrapes with the law, including a murder, and how he captured the hearts and curiosity of people wherever he roamed.

His story includes a murder and the resulting trial. Unfortunately, the transcript of the trial was not in the court's file, so I have relied on extensive newspaper accounts to piece together the events that transpired on a San Jose highway and the trial that followed. I have changed the names and characters of the victim and others so as not to intrude upon any living descendants.

Old Man
of
The Mountains

Chapter 1

The Pencil

Inside a deep crevice of a pocket of the purse was a 2" pencil stub. It had been tucked away and hidden inside the purse for more than 70 years. I clutch the old, worn pencil, which had been crudely sharpened with a pocketknife. Through my fingers I feel a part of history flowing through me. In some strange way, I feel connected to Peter Voiss, California's most notorious gold prospector of the 20th century. I feel I know him well and will call him Pete.

Pete wrote stories and poetry, with many of his writings in pencil; possibly *this* pencil.

The pencil is as worn as he was. Oh, if only it could talk. It was well-traveled and held by ancient, rough, and sweaty hands. Pete likely stuck it between yellowed, rotten teeth as thoughts of the next line of poetry ran through his head. As his aged eyes gazed upon the great outdoors, *his* outdoors, it appears that he had dug into the pencil's ridges with fingernails crusted with dirt, while thinking about the next story to write.

Imagine what it would be like riding down the highway and you see something ahead that needs a closer look. As the car approaches, you look over to the side of the road and see three gray burros pulling a canvas-covered makeshift cart. You peer over the side of the canvas and there he is. The tanned, wrinkled, old man has long gray hair and beard, with a large, sweat-stained hat perched on top of his head. His clothes are tattered and worn. The hands holding the reins are old, callused and as rough-looking as sandpaper. You wonder where he's been and where he's going, in this modern age of cars and tall buildings.

The pencil could tell you all about the life of the old prospector: How he lived in the mountains with nature and his burros--his best friends, and about all the places he's seen, from deserts to mountains, from mines to cities. The pencil could tell you about the hardships he faced as he made his way across California, about how people tried to take advantage of him, and how he protected himself. Perhaps the pencil could tell you what *really* happened on that spring day in 1936.

Pete was from a different time and place; he was unique, a non-conformist who lived a solitary life with his burros in the mountains. If asked about his address, he would tell you he lived "between the blue and the gold." Emigrating from Germany to America, and finally coming to California's Mother Lode and Bay Area, he touched people's lives when he came out of his mountains. He was a piece of California's rich Gold Country history, an eccentric old man with a fascinating story to tell.

Chapter 2

The "Find"

My father, George A. Heintz, was also a prospector of sorts, always looking for the end of the rainbow, as he tapped away at one mine or another. He had mining interests near Coulterville in Mariposa County and in other areas throughout California. Occasionally, he brought home rock samples such as Mariposite, dolomite, asbestos, and even a few gold nuggets. In 1950 he thought he'd found the elusive pot of gold at the end of the rainbow and wrote the following account about his "find:"

It was the spring of 1950. I was prospecting for a source of chrysotile asbestos in the serpentine ore group that stretched in the Mother Lode of California from Mariposa County in the south to Plumas County in the north. I had a lead that there was a serpentine asbestos find near an old mining community called Jenny Lind.

[Jenny Lind is located approximately 60 miles southeast of Sacramento. It is thought that the miners named the town in honor of the "Swedish Nightingale," Jenny Lind, who had toured the country with P.T. Barnum during Gold Rush days.]

After chipping rocks with my miner's hammer and keeping a few small specimens for further study, I was about to leave the vicinity when I spotted what looked like an old adit to a mine. Climbing up a short slope I came to the entrance. It was shored up with old railroad ties with no indication of rotting. I had to stoop a bit to enter but inside after a few feet I could stand upright. Snapping my flashlight on I noticed the stoop was covered with soot, indicating a fire at sometime. I'd progressed about twenty feet when I came to a dead end. There was evidence of a cave-in at this point.

It was real cool, probably 20 degrees cooler than outside. In one corner was a fire-charred press of branches. Hanging from a splinter from a railroad tie was what looked like a black woman's purse tied with a piece of rawhide. I had found a bonanza! A stash? Of what? My first thought was a miner's poke loaded with gold nuggets!

Frantically, I untied the rawhide that was secured around the purse. What was I to find? Nuggets? Gold coins? $100 bills?...Money, money, money! As I poured the contents on the ground outside in the light, gold coins did not drop out. "Oh my garsh!" I picked up the purse and trudged back through the brush in the direction of my car parked about a mile down the hill off a back road. I took off immediately. Was it finders, keepers?

As I drove along the dusty road I kept looking through my side view mirrors, until I got to the freeway. Then, and only then did I relax. What was I running from? Was I a thief? No. Finders, keepers. It eased my conscious.

It will always remain a mystery how that black purse tied with a piece of rawhide containing some of the last personal effects of Peter Voiss got stashed away in a mining shaft outside Jenny Lind, California.

This "find" took my father back to 1939 when he was a reporter for *The Tavern News*, a newspaper published by the Tavern Owner's Association of California located in San Francisco. He was assigned to cover the opening of the Golden Gate International Exposition, the World's Fair.

It was at this event that he further described his first encounter with the old man:

> *I first met Peter Voiss in July 1939 at the World's Fair in San Francisco on Treasure Island. His little canvas cart and three small jennies [burros] were parked on the east side of the island near the breakwater. He told me his "diggin' was up Feather River way.*
>
> *He was tall and lanky and substantially beyond middle age. He had a long white beard and lots of white hair that had gone limp and yellowish. As he spoke there was about a half-century of cigarettes and whisky in his voice. His face was packed full of creases and grey-brown shadows; two pale blue eyes peered at me underneath a beaten up, sooty, Stetson hat.*
>
> *"Ya wanna buy a postcard?" he yelled, "cost yer a dollar." He reached in the side pocket of his dirty jacket and handed me a postcard of himself and his jennies taken on that very spot on Treasure Island. I gave him a silver dollar; he took it and walked away without a thank you. Little did I know then that it would be more than a decade later that I would stumble upon some of the old prospector's most intimate possessions.*

The Press Pass George Heintz used to enter the World's Fair
in San Francisco

George Heintz prospecting in California's mountains,
ca 1950s

Although it wasn't the gold nuggets he had expected, the contents of the purse offered a glimpse into the life of a reclusive old man who years before had captured the headlines of the nation. For many years Pete had been a spectacle as he wandered California's highways and byways traveling with his beloved burros.

Pete managed to find a miner's cabin to stay in during part of the year, but for the most part, his home was his canvas-covered cart. He made his cart with three shafts in which the burros were hitched. He used a brake drum from an automobile and mounted it on one of the buggy wheels; the lever served as a carrier for his shotgun. The stock of the gun rose above the load and a rope attached to it enabled Pete to put on the brakes when needed.

With his cart his home, Pete's yard was made of the surrounding mountains and gulches, riverbeds and meadows. Gigantic ponderosa pine trees enveloped him and kept him safe, while hillsides of orange poppies and blue larkspur soothed his ancient eyes. The mountains' silence lulled him to sleep at night while he slept on California's green and gold.

When on the move, he carried all of his worldly possessions with him as he searched for gold throughout California's Mother Lode.

My father could easily relate to Pete. Both were free-spirited, intelligent, and rebellious old prospectors, who lived simply. And they were both dreamers. Understandably, when my father met Pete, he felt an unforgettable connection. Was it fate that he had found Pete's belongings? Whether or not fate lent a hand, the find set my father on a sporadic 37-year journey to learn more about the man he had met at the World's Fair. By the time he met him at the fair, he knew that the old guy was infamous. The incident in 1936 did not escape many people's attention, not even my father's, who at the time, was living in Great Falls, Montana.

You may be wondering: What was inside the old purse? Tucked securely inside were stories, photos, newspaper clippings about Pete's travels, and poems scratched on the backs of envelopes and pieces of paper. In 1955, my father published a story in *The Farm Tribune*, a Porterville, California newspaper, in which he sought the public's help in providing more information on the old prospector.

He imagined the replies he would get to the article, and he pondered about what his response to those replies would be. During his daydreaming, he lazily scrawled on a piece of paper what he would say to the people:

Isn't it odd that I should receive a communication from you about Peter

8

Voiss? Is it possible you have read or heard about him? By gorm, it's been near a decade or more since I searched for a party who would recognize the name. Yes, I have his last bequeath, secure in the same leather packet he carried with him with his donkeys, his original writings in pencil, some in ink....

He received just two responses. One was from Mrs. Alta May Crawford of Fresno. She replied that she had met Pete in 1940 while visiting her friend Mrs. Evans in San Francisco. They went out to see the old man and brought him some fruit.   Beyond that, she had no further information.

The other response was from a gentleman who referred him to a March 1936 issue of *National Geographic* magazine, which carried a colored picture of the prospector, his cart and burros.

Somewhat discouraged, he filed away his dreams and desires to do something with his find, and got on with life. It wasn't until the spring of 1987 that the desire that had only lain dormant erupted into my father's life with a vengeance.

He was sitting in his doctor's office in Auburn, California. He had sat in this room many times during his final illness, but on this particular day, he noticed a framed picture-postcard hanging on the wall behind him. The picture was of Pete with his cart and burros. My father got excited again, and as he told his doctor the story, his enthusiasm spread. Dr. Dolkas was intrigued and told his wife the story. She, in turn, wrote to my father, "Tell me more." They planned to discuss the contents of the purse, but my father's illness progressed and the meeting never took place.

Despite his illness, he decided to make one last attempt at finding more information about Pete. With the help of his friend and editor of the *Territorial Dispatch,* a small Meadow Vista, California, newspaper, he once again published an article asking anyone who had known the prospector to contact him. There wasn't a single response.

Now that his enthusiasm had been rekindled and with his disease progressing, I'm sure my father felt a sense of urgency to tell me the story. On our next visit, he brought the purse out of the drawer and removed its plastic wrap. The story of the purse he had found more than three decades before spilled from him, eager to be told. As he carefully unfolded the now-yellowed paper that Pete had written his stories on, he told me of his frustration at knowing he had a piece of history but hadn't been able to find out anything more about this mysterious old prospector. The story fascinated me and I decided I simply had to find out more about the old man who lived in the mountains.

The black purse and some of Pete's stories and other
documents; also the "pencil" Pete used to write his stories

The author with the black purse and some of Pete's pictures

Pete gets some help while panning for gold

Chapter 3

The Early Years

Peter Voiss was born sometime between 1862 and 1867, no one knows for sure, in a small village outside Cologne, Germany. Dates and days of the weeks meant nothing to Pete. His age and other references to time differ in the various accounts of his life.

He was born into a family of nine, the son of a small brewery and inn owner. Pete was very close to his mother and thought she was the most beautiful woman in the world. He learned about the finer things in life from his mother, including an appreciation for the works of Beethoven.

Although Pete lived a rather unconventional life after coming to America, he was well educated in his homeland, having attended the University of Bonn in Germany. He was well-versed in both Greek and Latin. He studied the works of poets Heinrich Heine and Friedrick Schiller, as well as the German writer Johann Wolfgang von Goethe.

While a student at the university, he wrote a poem that the Kaiser, William I, felt insulted Jesus. The Kaiser was a devout Christian and believed God destined him for the monarchy. This blasphemy threatened his political career. As punishment, he sentenced Pete to three months in Cologne's fortress. Pete later wrote that although he was imprisoned, the experience wasn't as bad as being in jail. He never felt any remorse for writing the poem: "I am proud of it; God gave me the inspiration." The poem, written in German and later translated into English, is not included here due to Pete's wishes that it not be published "under any circumstances."

Pete also studied merchandising at the university and was expected, after graduation, to find work as a clerk. However, that was not the kind of life for him; he just could not fulfill his parents' dream. He always preferred the wide-open spaces to the confines of city life. He loved the Rhineland so much that he never expected to leave it.

While at the university, Pete fell in love with a beautiful girl named Margaret. The romance lasted two years. She wanted to get married. He wasn't ready for a commitment, and she began to sense that he probably never would be.

Tired of waiting, Margaret confronted him, "Peter, I cannot wait for you. I have found someone else."

Heartbroken, Pete wanted to forget his pain, but more than anything he wanted adventure. He had heard about opportunities in America, especially opportunities to find gold. So with only a few marks in his pocket, he left for America, traveling by steerage. He left his family behind forever.

Peter Voiss is listed on the New York-bound passenger list, arriving and waving a hand at Miss Liberty, on October 25, 1893. He had departed from Antwerp, Belgium on the ship Westernland. His age is listed as 26 years, 11 months. On the ship's manifest, Pete is listed as a brewer. Not surprising, since his father owned a brewery, and he probably worked in his father's business.

After arriving in America and teaching himself English, he worked in factories for a couple of years throughout the East and South. But the call of the West beckoned him. He thought perhaps his brother Gottfreid, who had arrived in America five years before him, could help. In 1900, Gottfried was a druggist with the Alexian Brothers Hospital in Chicago, Illinois.

When Pete asked for his brother's help, Gottfried suggested he come to work for him in his store: "You will earn enough money for your travels."

Pete turned the offer down, knowing that that type of life was too confining for him. Instead, he took up mining and made his way out West without anyone's help, destined to live his life in the open air and beauty of the mountains.

The height of California's Gold Rush may have been during the middle of the 19th century, but the lure of the precious metal continued well into the 20th century. For those who were seeking riches beyond belief, the lure was strong, as strong as the metal itself. The end of the rainbow was always just on the other side of the mountain. And Pete itched to find it.

My first glimpse of the State told me that California would be my home always. It was mine from the first moment I looked upon it nearly half a century ago. I saw that it carried the same wild rugged beauty that my Rhineland carried, the same wooded slopes and graceful valleys.

Sacramento was the first city I went to upon my arrival. It was a wide-open town in those days, colorful and picturesque and crowded with miners who had money to spend.

Their names have escaped me, all except Petty's. Petty was a handsome Irish woman from County Kerry, who ran a hotel and a saloon, an opportunist who always wore a big black apron.

That apron of Petty's did her more good than either her hotel or her saloon. When her "boys," as she used to call them, drank themselves into a stupor on paydays, she saw to it that they were carried to their rooms feet first. It was then, while they were en route upstairs that Petty put her apron to use. She held it out, like a dark cloud, and caught whatever money fell from her "boys'" pockets.

I always felt I was pretty much of a disappointment to Petty. I was not a drinking man and therefore I left no trail of gold in that swishing apron of hers. [Reprinted with permission from the *San Francisco Chronicle*, July 5, 1936.]

Pete had learned a lot about the mining business when he lived in the East, so he put this knowledge to work as he quickly settled into mining camps throughout California's Mother Lode.

Chapter 4

Mining Years

Pete was a proud man and considered himself one of the best miners in the state. He felt a miner's success was based on his experience and knowledge of the ore, not whether or not he got lucky. He had the knowledge and the experience, though luck was evasive. He endured the hardship of working underground for many years, breaking just about every bone in his body. He nearly lost his life countless times due to cave-ins, which were a fact of a miner's life. A cave-in could happen unexpectedly at any time. Without his knowledge of the mines, Pete surely would have been killed.

In those days California's deepest mines were my home, the Empire, the North Star and many others. I hated working below the earth, working like a mole in constant darkness. I couldn't breathe, I couldn't see my sky. But I learned. And today, as I look back, I know that no fancy engineer, with a string of initials after his name, can beat me at mining.

Then Pete burst into song:

You see me trudging to some secret holes,
That yawn from out a rocky ledge I know
Close followed by my burros—faithful souls
Pick and pan clanking as we go

You know the hope that spurs my steady gait
At dawn, to isolated regions, where

19

A rocky trail and visions wait
And the hope that lives in ledges everywhere.

You hear my poor old voice hopefully blend
In conversation with this lonely hill
Whose lure I know and follow to my end
Where gold and minerals spill.

You know the trail that tortures,
And the pain
Of bended back and aching toiling hands
The drive of pick into the heartless vein
Somewhere surely God sees, and understands.

This is my song to the prospector. I sing it to him because I understand him. I understand the dream that sends him on. The weariness that gnaws at his heart and gives him fear.
I understand because for three-quarters of my life I have been a prospector. So this song is my song, too, and the things I have tried to address are the emotions I have known. [Reprinted with permission from the *San Francisco Chronicle*, July 5, 1936.]

Pete left California several times to try mining elsewhere. He had heard that there were some good strikes in Mexico, so he headed South. However, this venture went sour when everything he owned was stolen, even his shoes. Barefoot, he returned to California. He hadn't struck it rich in Mexico, but he had fooled the thieves out of his gold. The thieves were unaware that what little gold Pete did find was buried in the ground. There wasn't enough to bother to return for it, so there it remained in the ground.

Burying gold was a practice that many miners and prospectors resorted to. Pete had buried tools, picks and shovels, and even a little gold at various claims in California, including Plumas County. He had always intended to return to his claims, so he kept a map of his burial spots. Unfortunately, he hadn't kept them in the black purse. It wouldn't have mattered, though. Pete made sure that only he could read 'em! Had there been a map, my father surely would have made an attempt to find his pot of gold.

After the 1906 earthquake in San Francisco, Pete, along with hundreds of other miners, was called upon to clear out a railroad tunnel a mile-and-half long. The men were lying on their backs with candles on long sticks cleaning the tunnel when several temblors hit. They all feared for their lives as the tunnel gave way and tons of rocks came crashing down around them. The weight of the debris crushed Pete's toes. It's a wonder he and the rest of the men got out alive.

By 1910, Pete was in Alameda County, California. The 1910 census for the City of Alameda, dated April 25, 1910, lists Pete as a boarder with William and Evelyn Montijo. His occupation is listed as a miner in the gold industry.

This is the only census year that Pete had a real address and could be accounted for. In 1920 and 1930 he is not found. The outdoors and his cart and burros were his home and family, far away from man's influence.

Working 5,000 feet underground was a dangerous way of life, with cave-ins a constant threat. Bosses were relentless as they drove the miners to work harder and harder without any regard for their safety. The hours were long, 14-16 hours a day, and the pay was low, $3.50 a day at the most.

Around 1915, Pete left the mining camps where he was under the proverbial thumb of his boss, a position that he never liked. Wanting some freedom, he and another miner became partners, forming the "Hall and Voiss Mine" in Belden, Plumas County, California. A sheet of the mine's stationery was found among Pete's belongings. Copper was commonly found in the mines of Plumas County, but it was the possibility of gold that called to old prospectors like Pete. No one can be sure how long this mining business lasted, but it's easy to imagine that Pete simply decided one day to pick up some wild burros, sever the mining venture with Hall, and strike out on his own. No doubt he would rather work with his burros than other people; many times he said that his burros were his best friends, and the most faithful of creatures.

My Burros or Donkeys!

Peter Voiss

The donkey is the most faithful animal (except the dog) who carried our Saviour through Jerusalem Street and is the most misunderstood animal.

Asinaes (Latin) we call an expression asnine, what stupid as nevertheless I will show my readers soon that there is always a reason why they want not to do things you order. They are so intelligent smart you are surprised.

They are liable to fool you anytime. Nearly everything in animal life you can learn them, they never forget a trail, a road, a house wherever they stopped. Sometimes I had objection to feed them sweets, etc. I know if I passed again they walk right in. I had many of them whenever I ceased or had to cease prospecting I turned them loose somewhere where plenty food and water was to enjoy liberty. I never scold them. I believe that would be the most precious deed for man and animal liberty, liberty blue and gold.

They all are great lovers, great beggars for food, great pets. They never are vicious except when they are treated bad, hit or teased. They naturally then kick object or bite.

I have one now. As I got that good jenny "Trixy." She was nervous, hard to catch, did not want to be petted. Today she is the most trustful animal in the mountains, never strips her pack, careful stopped, on step and dangerous places on the trail, unafraid to cross creeks and rivers.

I crossed the Yuba, the American River dozens of times with my wagon. As I crossed the last time the American River, an incident happened, that I cannot to figure out how smart they are (every word is true).

I came below Applegate to the river with my cart and the 3 burros. Doctor, the little stallion burro, was 10 months old. I left him tied up. We crossed with 2 burros and the cart through 18-20 inches of water, rough gravel bottom reaching a bar, and I unhitched, put my rubber boots on, took the two burros Jimmy (Meboy), Trixy (Megirl) to get Doctor. I had a ¾ inch but long rope. I took a hitch back to Doc's shoulder blade, let the end come through front legs, through his halter, and fastened to end. Trixy tugs to pull Doc. Jimmy was looking on.

Doctor would not come. Before I could give Trixy orders to pull, Jimmy came up and took Doc by the nose and pulled him. I told Jimmy to let Doc's nose loose. He did. Doc tried to lay down feeling the water raised and we all crossed like old-timers.

As I observed this action Jimmy, like human, wanted Doc to obey my orders and I learned that the point of the nose is the vital spot to force orders.

Nevertheless, Doc followed me alone through the river. Next day whenever I crossed the river Doc watched me and follow me. It was a pretty sight. The little fellow in that deep water, wherever I worked he came to see me, such a good companion. I could see long before whenever somebody was coming over the trail or through the brush on his ears. Whenever I could not see the burros, I called Doctor. He bayed and runned up to me. Doctor likes beer. One time before a parade, he drank 5 bottles. They lay in mountains at nights close to my tent. It is an awful fine picture! They play and fight.

Would you not love them who divide life with you in such faithful manner?

Doctor was an awful fighter, for he killed 2 dogs and crippled 7. In his younger days someone told me a dog was the cause he got hurt in barbwire fence. He never forgot that. One day Doc tore my only blanket to pieces.

He bit and kicked and when I took him out he walked sometimes on the hind feet. Anyway, when he kicked, I did not know if the front or hind feet were on the ground, getting life. The rascal one day got into my grubbox. As I came back what a mess. Everything torn up. Coffee, all the sugar, flour, macaroni, butter, eggs, bacon, etc., gone. Even at that I could not punish him. I loved him so much. It was my fault. I ought to be carefuller. I could not hold him on a rope. He chewed the rope off and rope off the other burros too. I had a chain and sprung that with his neck, strong. He bit me several times, went in my pocket to get chewing tobacco, tore the pocket off on my mackinaw [a heavy woolen blanket].

Today you see him, the best animal I ever had. I know his faults and give him no show. Whatever, he knows his master loves him. Anyone can pet him now. Mrs. D. raised Doctor on the bottle. It was her pet. Later I broke him and Mrs. D. gave it to me. Lately the lady could not have him around her home; he pranced through the neighbor's flowers.

One time I was prospecting on a place 5 miles off my cabin. It was in Sept. It got dark on me. I had one burro along, "Mary." I had only few tools so I took the saddle off and did lay down to sleep. Too dark to go to cabin. The saddle for the pillow, my coat, saddle blanket over me. I froze, I raised up, put the saddle on her, and said to myself, I take a chance on you to bring me to the cabin. The trail was rough and 500 feet above the riverwall, straight up. I took a hold on her tail and she good animal took me to the cabin. They see in the dark better than human, they want no lights.

Some other time I packed out I make 5 trips to the road over the trail. The 6th trip I had a pump about 180 lb. on her as we was 200 feet on the mountainside. She kneel *down and over she went, pump, burro rolled over rocks and brush in the canyon. I went down.*

She had her eyes closed and grinning. I thought she was hurt to die now. I took the pack (pump) off. She had her head on some pine oak. She did not like that. She shook her head. Oh, I said to myself, you want to fool me. I went and got a little stick. She saw me comin up. Mary runned off up the hill. I cut her way off and said to her, come on, you forgot something: to take the pump up and she carried the pump. Whenever the burros fail to stop they do this trick: kneel down and rolled. They never get hurt. They make a living where a goat dies. In heat, snow, they want no stall. They want to be free. One time I was caught in snowstorm 2 feet snow. The burros were underneath a big oak tree. I had only 6 lb. grain left, no hay. I cut branches off the tree and they did eat all of it. They did not want to be inside, but to be free.

Many times they tramped through a foot of snow, but there is one thing they always think that they are wiser than you. They do not stay in the middle of the road. They try the sides and fall in chuckholes. A weary travel, no use to pull the lines, just let them find out, leave them alone and OK.

I was working on a small quartz ledge. I washed that morning early and when the burros were around, and I did not watch out every time, they drink the soapwater and I had to go and get new water. They had a creek full water but they preferred soapsuds.

I hanged all my wash on the line. I went to my work. As I came back they had all my underwear chewed to pieces.

I went 4 miles back, up the hill and told a miner's wife my plight. The lady told me she could let me have some underwear. She went in the house and came out with a package. I thank her very much for the help out.

I walked 4 miles back, as was in my cabin. I wanted to put the underwear on. A lady's union suit here my trouble started. I tried to put the feet in. I could not get the arms in. I put the arms in. I could not get the feet in. Silencia.

I laid it on the floor and studied how the ladies put that thing on, a song to me. I saw a little string on the collar and I opened it, widened it out—aha, that means feet first and pull up. I was proud and some way bashful that I did not had any prior experience. Everytime the lady in question meet me asked me how about a union suit?

So I come back to my story. I put Mary in some good pasture across the creek a mile from my cabin (in the same canyon). In about a week Mary came to my cabin, her body swollen, her eyes red, her mouth full of slime. She insisted to come in. I saw she was sick. I no medicine. I took a pound of common salt, put it in bottle with little water and put down her throat. She lay down underneath a tree. I surely thought she go to die. After 10 minutes she raised up, kicked a few times, and went off to the pasture, didn't even say thanks. How this animal know I help her? It never came before. There is a reason—what I cannot dissolve yet.

Trixy never had any shoes on before, so I put shoes on Jimmy. Trixy was alongside. I thought I would have a hard time. I had her shoes ready. I asked her for the foot and put the shoes on. If she has a rock in her foot or lost a shoe she lifts the foot up to show me? Reason? There is no animal except a dog and elephant who are so smart.

Slow but sure they are awful careful when they step not in a hole, on a root on a sewer man hole, on an iron plate, on bridges, on rock points, they avoid all. Reason?

I had a donkey. We had to pass over a cable (narrow bridge over a creek). Everytime it look down and over every plank, I guess it wanted to see that carpenter did not forget any nails. In the middle of the bridge if it shake a little, I never seen an animal so frightened as it was shaking all over everything. Reason?

I could write a big book. Now I give you a little story of Meboy, a 950 lb. donkey. I drove him without any bridle with a pack on from the Ferry over Market Street to City Hall in N.S. parade. I walked 4 steps back of him, he watched my signals.

He never had heard a radio and a radio played in house and he walked on the sidewalk to listen. He would not move. A patrolman came and told me to get him off the sidewalk. I told him the best thing to do would be that he go in the house and stop the radio to let us pass. Reason?

Accidents. I had quite a few. I was camping in a hole along the highway; plenty good feed was there. As drop out I walked and we had quite 150 yards to go to the highway. As I was on the highway a ways opposite my camping place, I left just before, I boarded the cart—the burros took the beeline back into the hole, my cart, donkeys, me all rolled into the hole. Broke 2 beams. I had nitric acid with me; it spilled all over groceries and blankets. I hurt my hand and arm. I did do the repairs but as I left I boarded my cart way past the good pasture. There was a heavy snow. I took Meboy in my cabin, but oh no, I could not leave him in there. He ate the wallpaper off, etc.

Another time in Butte County I passed over a washed out road. I filled the roadway in with my shovel and try to pass over, but the burros backed and the cart fell in the deep hole. This was on a hillside in loose decomposed granite. Trixy was in the hole. I loosened Jimmy; he got out, but Trixy was loosened too, but slid underneath the axle of the cart (here we come to reason again). I got the shovel to dig her out; she bit in shovel handle. Did it mean hurry up or was she to help me? I dug *and dug to make room for her to come out. She was still under the axle. The only salvation was to throw the cart over and I broke the wheel. I took bedding and food for 4 days and traveled 28 miles in the valley to find new wheels, leaving the cart and other stuff behind. I rode Jimmy— Trixy packed—it took me 3 days. I found an axle and new (poor) wheels, then I went back 28 miles to pick the wreck up. I had to take the axle off and put the new underneath a whole day's work—10 miles from anybody—I had to do it alone, some tough lifting. Where there is will there is way.*

One day Meboy, the big donkey who got crippled in smashup on the highway in '32 had a pack on, about 200 lb. and in a town he laid down. Yes, for rest, but mind you, middle on the main street. A policeman came up and said to let us drag him towards the sidewalk; that the cars can pass. OK, I said, and I got a hold on the front feet. The policeman took a hold on the hind feet. A big crowd was there. Yes, the policeman never will touch the hind feet no more. Meboy kicked him and the crowd roaring with laughter. And he told me as we both pulled Meboy off the street to get him up. I told him I could not hurry him. I had to talk to him first. Now, hurry, get him up! Oh, hold your horses. I whispered to Meboy in the ear the saying out the Bible (the same I done him something nobody saw). My son raise up, and up he went. More than 100 people around yelling. The show was over.

Meboy did not care to roll on a hillside. He never got hurt. I learned him to open a door, so one evening we were invited to stop camp in the yard. Meboy was loose. He went to the back door, opened it, the lady came towards the door. Meboy said mm mm, what is the matter with the donkey, sick? No, I said, he wants something to eat. I learned him to open the door, but not to beg.

I was working in a gulch. I put a pot of beans (strawberry) on the fire. I came back at dinner; the donkey had thrown the pot of beans off the fire and had eaten my beans.

One time he runned off with 25 lb. sack of flour, he dropped it when he saw me coming.

A man has to be careful. They steal whenever they have a show.

They examine every box. Jimmy can open a trunk; he works on the middle, lifts the top, but does not put his nose in. Too wise, afraid the sharp rim, kicks it.

They eat all the labels off the cans paper. Doc bites the rope off. They like Leslie's tomato hot sauce; it must be good if the donkeys like it. They like orange, lemon peelings. Jimmy picks once a while a cigar; he smoke up. I told him be careful or he may get pinched.

Jimmy was a year ago stolen from me. I guess he was gone about a month (I have not and need no calendar). One night he came back to me. I know he would. I promised him honey and sugar if I could afford it the rest of my life.

When the sun rises they wake me up. Everyone gets a big hot cake. They never miss the time.

I could write much more, but I wrote the most vital points of these faithful souls who are man's best companions. I ride life and hardship with him. Hardships, hunger, rain, snow, heat, no home can stand. They are tough in one word. They make about 18-20 miles a day. When I put them in high, I make 48 miles a day—the best—(from Oakland to Tracy).

I care for my companions in the best way.

Pete's best friends, his burros, take time out for a photo

Chapter 5

The Roaring Twenties

Away from the mines and their filthy camps, Pete began wandering with his faithful burros into areas outside his California mountains. He loved the thrill of prospecting, and in his search for the metal, he traveled into Death Valley and parts of the West into Utah, Idaho and Nevada. However, he loved the beauty of California's Feather River area the best, and returned to California and his mountains.

World War I, the "war to end all wars," had just ended, and the 1920s brought prosperity and optimism to the nation. The "Roaring Twenties" brought hemlines up and women's hair was cut shorter. It was the era of Al Capone and Prohibition. There were movies, and a new invention called radio to keep people informed and entertained. It was the decade of the $5 day, the Model T, and the first transatlantic flight that made Charles Lindbergh famous. Pete was happily oblivious of it all. His mountains sheltered him as he lived day by day always searching for gold.

The Prospector
Peter Voiss

Far away—the mountains of golden dream
The burros with saddle and pack will trod
Mystic hope and desire—like fire agleam
Soon the gray mountain where silence is broad.

Eager looking and looking for gold
The fever—that's the pride of the game
Steady hammering the drill—quick and bolt.
Is it failure or success—all the same
Not count hardship or time spent
The lure of gold that makes content.

Cussing the parasite and the pimp
Heartless are luck and strife
Hardened to the bone and not a simp
It's the game in human life
Crowned be—who knows no defeat
Blast the round—my strike a lead.

Shows sulphides—yellow, blue, black
Ripping deeper in the guts of quartz
Looks not bad—may carry a golden flake
Works and picks till hands smart
Not in day or year may he win
A piece as big as the head of a pin.

Deeper, deeper he delves into the core
That he may strike some milling ore
Another round—but hard is the ground
And he sings—as the hammer's blow rings
If confidence and skill don't decline
O Lord some day he strikes a mine.

Surely, it must be not in vain
Or his bones may stake his claim
Ahead with bull's determination
Or he strikes prospector's pension

Poverty

Pete with his burros

Chapter 6

Depression Years

The 1930s brought the Great Depression, which followed the stock market crash of October 29, 1929. Many people suffered severe losses in the stock market, and when the market improved slightly during the 1930s, people were reluctant to spend their money. Unemployment was high and those in the mining business were equally affected.

Pete didn't believe in banks, preferring to bury his gold in Mother Earth. For him, the earth was the safest bank in the world. "It will never fall," he asserted.

Many out-of-work men left their homes and families trying to find work wherever they could. Some rode on trains to their destinations of "nowhere in particular;" others hiked their way around the country looking for a family that would take them in for the night, give them a bite of food for their starving bellies, and in return they'd do chores on the farm. These hobos, as they were known, were out there traveling around the country, right alongside Pete. However, this wasn't a new way of life for Pete. He was familiar with the vagabond life and had grown accustomed to the hardships that accompany it. The significant difference between Pete and the rest of the hobos was that Pete was an object of curiosity with his cart and his burros. He made news wherever he went.

By the 1930s Pete was competing with more and more automobiles on the highways. He and his cart and burros were quite a sight as they made their way out of the mountain gulches in the springtime and slowly traveled down the roads into the cities. He was trying to eek out a living just like the men on the road with him.

He managed to use his straggly appearance to his advantage. After all, he was the real deal, an honest-to-goodness, California gold prospector. He truly looked the part. Where there were tourists, you were likely to find Pete, carrying gold nuggets to show off and proudly answering their questions. If they begged him, he might just let them buy a nugget or two.

When Pete was prospecting for gold in the 1920s, the price was averaging $20.71 an ounce. By 1931, the price had plummeted to $17.06 an ounce and rose again in 1932. When Pete visited the Ott Assay office in Nevada City, California, in February of that year, he had his gold nuggets weighed and tested for purity before the pay out of $20.69 an ounce.

The price began to rise in the mid-1930s reaching $34.86 an ounce in 1936. By this time, however, Pete was pushing 70 years, and it was becoming harder and harder to find enough of the gold flakes to make a living. He began to think of ways to supplement his income. At last he had it! People wanted his photo, and in 1934 were offering him 25 cents to have his picture. He gladly accepted, and this became his way of making a living for himself and his burros.

Pete could be seen in and around the cities of Tracy, Turlock, Oakland, Hayward, San Jose, Los Gatos, Santa Cruz, Watsonville and Gilroy. When he wasn't camping out in the mountains, he would camp out of sight of civilization on the cities' outskirts. He frequently camped along the cliffs of Santa Cruz where he sold rides on his burros to the children in the area. He let them ride a quarter of a mile for just a nickel.

It was these adored Santa Cruz mountains and a determined motorist that would haunt Pete in the coming weeks.

Chapter 7

Stop, or I'll Shoot!

Thursday, April 23, 1936 began like any other spring day in San Jose, California. It was a cool, breezy morning with the temperature expected to reach a warm 65 degrees by mid-afternoon. Cherry, apricot, and plum trees flourished in their orchards with bountiful crops expected during the summer. Children's voices echoed in the distance as they played in their schoolyards. Unknown to the busy folks in town, two people from two very different worlds were about to meet and bring this Bay Area city into the spotlight.

Thirty-three-year-old Franklin Darcey was just finishing up with his last client of the morning in his Morgan Hill office. He stamped out his cigarette, and standing up, his tall, stocky frame loomed over his desk as he shook his client's hand in departure. He was a successful attorney and had recently opened up a second office in San Jose. Feeling pleased with himself, he was looking forward to a full calendar of appointments in his San Jose office that afternoon. It was nearly noon when he grabbed his coat from the hook near the window. Glancing out the window, he caught a glimpse of Pete and his burros as they passed through town.

He thought to himself, "If I hurry, I can catch up with that old guy and get that picture of him and his donkeys." He gave his secretary, Helen Wicks, last minute instructions. "I'll see you tomorrow. Call me if you need anything." He shut the door to his office and got in his car--a brand-new 1936 Chevrolet 4-Door Touring Sedan.

As he pulled out of the parking lot, he thought about his three young daughters, Virginia, 6, Martha, 4, and Dorothy, 2.   Grinning to himself, he thought about Virginia, who had lost her first tooth that morning. The tooth fairy must remember to bring her a nickel tonight.

He headed down the Monterey highway towards his San Jose office when he came upon the prospector and his burros. Darcey was an amateur photographer and was determined to get a picture of them. He had tried to get a picture of the old guy and his burros three weeks before; he had been driving through the Santa Cruz mountains, but Pete chased him away with his shotgun.

The bearded man and his cart were ahead of Darcey's car about 100 yards. The attorney stopped his car to grab his camera from the glove box. Meanwhile, a car pulled up and stopped in front of his car. It was his old friend Deputy Andrew Day. Day had recognized the car as Darcey's. He'd shown it off to his friend over the past weekend. Day walked back to the car and tapped on the window, "Anything wrong, Frank?"

Darcey rolled down the window. "Nothing's wrong, Andy, just adjusting my camera. I want to get a picture of that old man and his burros ahead." After chatting a bit, Day returned to his car, and rejoined his partner, Deputy Fred Marshall. The pair had picked up a 13-year old car thief in Hollister and were transporting him to San Jose.

Pete and his cart were pulled off to the side of the road next to a cherry orchard where he was feeding his burros some of the snails he'd bought that morning in Watsonville. Darcey's car pulled around the deputies' car, driving up next to the cart. He pulled too close, though, and the burros shied; one of them broke away.

Pete reached out and grabbed the loose burro, his hat flying off his head. In all the turmoil, he looked up and recognized the occupant of the car. It was the same guy he had run off a few weeks before for trying to take his picture. He had written down the license plate number on the label of his ragged sweater and had planned to report him to the highway patrol for harassing him. Pete was becoming increasingly angry that he wasn't being paid for the pictures that photographers, both commercial and amateur, were taking of him. He was supposed to be paid 25-50 cents for the privilege of taking his picture. This supplemented his meager prospecting income.

The attorney drove ahead of Pete and his cart, pulled to a stop, and got out of his car. Quickly, he snapped a picture of the rig from a distance. With all the commotion, Pete was as nervous as his burros. He was all thumbs as he tied the little burro to the larger burros.

After taking the picture, the attorney threw his car in reverse and sped backwards, zigzagging until the car stopped beside the cart.

Pete was mad as hell and shook his fist at the attorney. Undaunted, Darcey slowly began to move forward again, bringing his camera up to take another picture. Pete grabbed his shotgun that was on the seat of the cart. The shotgun was an antique with a three-foot barrel and charred stump that had been used to put out campfires. He used it for protection while on the road, and well, he thought it completed the "look" of an old prospector.

Pete warned the attorney, "Stop, or I'll shoot!"

Determined to get a better picture, Darcey laughed at Pete's threat, defiantly calling back, "I'm gonna take your picture anyway!" The camera clicked, the car moved forward, and the shotgun went off. Buckshot smashed through the rear window and struck the attorney in the head. Darcey lost control as the car rolled to the left side of the road and into a ditch.

Darcy and Pete's clash happened in a matter of seconds, right in front of the two police officers and their prisoner. Marshall got out of his car and ran over to Darcey's car. He was alive, barely, so Marshall moved him over the blood-soaked seat and got behind the wheel. He would drive Darcey to the hospital.

A woman passerby ran to the car, calling out, "Can I do anything to help?"

"No," came the reply, "just get back in your car. There are plenty of men here to help." He paused. "Wait. You got a blanket?" The woman ran back to her car to retrieve a blanket. Marshall snatched the blanket from the woman and wrapped it around the attorney's bloody head.

Meanwhile, Day had run over and grabbed Pete, handcuffing him. Pete was dazed and confused, so didn't resist. "Don't you know that you just shot a man?" Day yelled at Pete. He threw him into the squad car with the other prisoner, turned on the siren, and escorted Marshall and Darcey, badly bleeding, to the San Jose Hospital.

Franklin Darcey was rushed into surgery where doctors removed five shots, slightly smaller than buckshot, from his head and brain. It wasn't enough. The bright, young attorney died at 7 o'clock that evening with his wife of seven years, Katherine, at his side.

The tooth fairy didn't visit little Virginia that night. Instead, the family was left in sorrow with a funeral to plan. Franklin Darcey, a successful attorney with a promising future ahead and a passion for photography, was laid to rest in Los Gatos Memorial Park in San Jose on Monday, April 27.

Pete was in a lot of trouble. He was initially locked up in the San Francisco City jail because the Santa Clara County Sheriff was home with the flu and didn't want him at the county jail until he could be in the office. Furious that the old man had killed his friend, Deputy Day kicked the 72-year old man in the back as he shoved him into his jail cell. "I'll kill you!" he shouted.

A dejected Pete shortly after his arrest

Overcome by the afternoon's events, Pete fainted in his jail cell. Weary and bewildered, he refused to talk with anyone until one of California's best known psychiatrists, Dr. E. W. Mullen of Agnews State Hospital examined him. He opened up and told the doctor that he was angry that people had been taking his picture without paying for them;

this income was needed for his and his burros' survival. Upon initial examination, Dr. Mullen felt the eccentric old man was "hopelessly insane," but admitted that further examination would be needed before a final determination could be made.

His three burros, Jimmy, Doc and Trixy, were left to wander the highway until they were brought to a corral in Coyote, near Morgan Hill, for the night. The next day they were transported to Auburn where they were corralled on property owned by Pete's good friend, and the donkeys' owner, Dr. Walter Durfee. Pete had been worried about his burros and their care until he learned that his dear donkeys were with his good friend. Here they would be well cared for.

Pete's rickety cart was taken to the county jail where officers combed through its contents. They found old clothing and a trunk that held some flour for making hotcakes, a little lard, some coffee, and some rusty tools. Hidden deep inside the trunk was the purse that held his most intimate possessions, including some stories and poems that he had written about his life. Pete had a mere $3.50 in his possession.

Pete told Prosecutor Charles McDonnell that he was angry when the attorney came by and raised his camera to take a picture. He'd had to chase off the same guy a few weeks before and now he was back to take his picture without paying for it. He was furious. Deciding he'd had enough, he "just had to shoot him," he told the prosecutor. Pete was charged with first-degree murder.

Within 24 hours, the prosecution had filed the murder complaint. The complaint stated that Peter Voiss "did unlawfully and feloniously kill and murder Franklin Darcey, a human being, with malice aforethought." He was remanded to the Santa Clara County Sheriff and held without bail.

Dr. Durfee and his wife, still caring for Pete's burros, traveled from Auburn to San Jose to visit their jailed friend. The Durfee's had met Pete five years before when he had come into Auburn with two aged burros and another very sick one. Durfee was a mild-mannered man, always willing to help a guy out. He was an optometrist who had practiced for many years in Auburn, and was a highly regarded member of the community. He recognized Pete as a man in need. Wanting to help, he took Pete under his wing and gave him three fresh burros, while pasturing and caring for the other burros. They would remain in his care for the rest of their lives.

Now their friend was facing a murder charge, and the Durfee's came to his side. "Don't worry about the donkeys, Pete. They're with us," Dr. Durfee assured the old man.

"Dat is goot. I vas worried," Pete told them. Overwhelmed, he looked to his friends, "I only try to scare the man; somehow the gun went off."

"We believe you, Pete. Don't worry," Durfee said, trying to comfort Pete. "We'll stand by you throughout this horrible ordeal." Pete gave a sigh of relief, grateful for their support.

Pete and his team coming into town

Chapter 8

The Trial

The preliminary hearing was set for May 6, with Judge Miller presiding. It was standing room only as spectators lined the walls of the courtroom to get a look at the wrinkled, old man accused of killing one of San Jose's most respected businessmen. Both Deputies Day and Marshall recounted the incident separately, as did the young prisoner they were transporting to jail at the time. All three related essentially the same story.

During the testimony, the court was interrupted when a woman spectator fell in a faint as she listened to the graphic descriptions of the murder. The judge called for a recess while the woman and the friends who assisted her were escorted from the courtroom.

The hearing soon resumed and Judge Miller ordered Pete to answer to superior court without bail.

Pete spent the next nine days sitting in his 5- by 9-foot jail cell restlessly waiting for the next step in the judicial process: his plea. He met with his attorneys a couple of times, as well as his old friends, the Durfee's. He complained to his friends that, "the light bulb over my head is on all night. I cannot sleep. I try to shade with piece of cardboard, but does not work good." His back was still hurting him a month after Day had kicked him. Forced to take his meals while kneeling on the floor, Pete's aging body constantly ached.

He tried to write a poem or two, but it was too difficult to concentrate. He missed his burros, and especially his freedom. He wished this whole thing had never happened; he wanted it over with, and soon.

49

On May 15, Peter Voiss appeared before the Honorable William Dunn, Judge, represented by his attorneys N. J. Menard, John D. Foley, and D. C. Kirby. Charles McDonnell represented the District Attorney.

Pete entered a plea of not guilty due to insanity at the time of the alleged murder, and the trial was set to begin on June 16, 1936 at 10:00 a.m. Because of the plea, not guilty by reason of insanity, the Judge appointed Dr. E. W. Mullen of Agnews State Hospital in Santa Clara and Dr. C. Kelly Cannel of San Jose to examine the defendant in order to determine his sanity.

At long last, the trial began. Pete was dressed in blue overalls and a khaki-colored flannel shirt, ready to sit through the jury selection process. Tired and pale, he passed the hours scribbling on a pad of paper or looking at the judge. Although the death penalty would not be sought, Pete confided to his attorney during a recess that he would prefer death over having to "sit in a cage the rest of his life".

By the end of the second day, a jury of six men and six women had been selected: Five fruit farmers, five housewives, one auto supply dealer and one nurse.

The third day of the trial included testimony from:

- Jim Johnson, Deputy Surveyor, who had drawn a detailed map of the murder scene.
- Dr. Stephen D'Ano, who attended the mortally wounded attorney.
- O. E. Price and Randall Price, who photographed the murder scene and the attorney's car.
- Leonard Fowler, a *Mercury Herald* cameraman who developed the film inside the attorney's camera, finding two pictures of Voiss.

- Rolland Samson, the 13-year-old car thief being transported to San Jose, who testified that he saw the old man hold the shotgun at his side and fire.

John Foley, Pete's lead attorney, contended that Pete had a run-in with the victim three weeks before on the Santa Cruz highway. "The deceased tormented my client when he tried to take his picture against his wishes. When Mr. Voiss encountered the deceased again on the road south of San Jose on April 23, he was more than a little annoyed."

He further stated, "When Mr. Voiss grabbed his shotgun, he intended to shoot at the car's tires. However, before he could raise the gun to his shoulder, the gun fired prematurely, hitting him in the elbow and bruising it. That bruise will prove that my client did not intend to shoot the victim."

However, Pete wasn't examined until a month after the shooting. The doctor testified that he didn't remember seeing a bruise.

The defense also brought forth two witnesses who testified they had seen the incident on the Santa Cruz highway three weeks before. Both Mr. and Mrs. Sam Walker stated that they had seen the attorney tease Pete while trying to take his picture. The defense intended to prove that the old man had been tested beyond endurance when he encountered the attorney on April 23.

In an attempt to discredit the young eye witness' testimony, the defense called upon Oliver Renton. Renton testified that at the preliminary hearing the young eyewitness, Rolland Samson, had related to him that the deputies had given him a story to tell, but he didn't know whether to tell that story or to tell the truth.

Another Eyewitness?

During the noon break on June 24, Prosecutor McDonnell returned to his office to check on his telephone messages. He had a message that he made sure to return right away. It was news that he hoped would help his case.

When court resumed in the afternoon, McDonnell stood up and faced the judge. "Your Honor, it has come to my attention that there is a fourth eyewitness to the murder. I respectfully request a continuance of the proceedings, as I need a few days to locate the witness."

Loud gasps could be heard in the courtroom. This was shocking news.

The judge called a recess so he could meet privately with both the defense attorneys and prosecutor in his chambers. The courtroom was abuzz with speculation as to who the witness could be.

Inside the chambers, McDonnell related that the witness' son had contacted him. The eyewitness was his mother. She had stopped to help after the shooting and had given a blanket to a man so he could wrap it around the man who'd been shot. Both Marshall and Day confirmed that a woman had stopped that day to help. Marshall also confirmed that he had borrowed a blanket from a woman passerby.

The court granted a continuance until the following Monday, July 1. Testimony resumed with the testimony of Mrs. Barbara Silverman of Bakersfield, the purported fourth eyewitness. She stated she'd been visiting her son in Palo Alto when she drove up behind the old man and his burros on the Monterey highway.

"I had been following a couple of cars and was about 10 feet from Mr. Voiss and his burros," she explained. "That old man over there [pointing to Pete] was really mad. I saw him lift his gun to his shoulder, aim and fire a shot at the man in the car."

She further stated, "I stopped and got out of my car to see if I could help. A man told me he didn't need any help, but he asked me if I had a blanket." She identified a bloodstained, brown blanket as the one she had given the man.

Both Deputies Day and Marshall testified they didn't remember seeing any other car at the precise time of the shooting. Voiss, himself, stated there were no other cars around during the actual shooting.

Another passerby, Francis Martin, testified that he came upon the scene shortly after the shooting and he didn't see Mrs. Silverman's car. He did, however, state that he heard Pete say, "I didn't mean to shoot him. I only meant to scare him."

Pete's Story

During the afternoon of July 1, Pete took the stand to testify on his own behalf. It was 85-degrees outside, but felt more like 95-degrees inside due to the many spectators crowded into the tiny courtroom. The room was stuffy, and Pete took a sip of water before he nervously walked to the stand. He spoke haltingly in broken English, but as he gained confidence, he relaxed and spoke more clearly.

He told the court that he was on his way to Auburn on the fateful morning of April 23 when the man approached him in his car, frightening him and his burros. He explained how one of the burros had broken away; that he grabbed her and tried to tie her to the other two burros while trying to settle all three. He went on to describe that the man in the car insisted on taking his picture against his wishes.

"I got my gun. I was nervous and the gun fired. I don't know how. I only meant to shoot the tires and scare the man away," he sobbed. He put his head in his hands, his shoulders shaking while continuing to sob. After composing himself, Pete looked up and pointed to Deputy Day. "That man pointed a gun at me and put handcuffs on me. He swore at me and threw me into front seat of a car. He didn't even search me," Pete said. "Just threw me into the car," he repeated.

"I tell the truth. No matter what witnesses say. I tell the truth."

When asked why he didn't report the incident in the Santa Cruz mountains to the highway patrol three weeks before, Pete responded, "I decided to forgive the man, then I forgot all about the incident."

As Pete left the stand, he apologized to the shorthand reporter, "Excuse my English. I did not go to American school."

Defense attorney Foley looked at the jury. "I don't believe for one minute that the only conversation that took place between the deceased, Franklin Darcey, and Deputy Andrew Day was that the deceased was preparing to take a picture of the old man and his burros," Foley charged. "I believe that Andrew Day wanted in on the fun of getting some great pictures!"

Foley went on to slam Day for telling a witness to lie, referring to Rolland Samson's testimony.

Foley concluded, "A man's home is his castle and he has a right to protect it. In this case, the old man's cart was his home and his castle, and he had a right to protect his home and his property."

As the trial came to a close, McDonnell told the jury that the prosecution was not excusing Mr. Darcey for bothering Voiss. "However," he explained, "the defendant had no right to take a human life. Because of this, the State had to file a murder charge. It is up to you, the jury, to decide whose testimony was relevant and true in this trial."

During concluding remarks, a commotion erupted in the courtroom. An old bearded man, who looked strikingly like Pete, stood up. "Free the old man!" he shouted before storming out of the courtroom.

Deliberation

After 11 days of testimony and nearly three weeks, it was time for the jury to decide Pete's fate. It wasn't going to be simple, and Judge Dunn wanted the jury to understand the job that lay before them. He spent 45 minutes giving them instructions.

He explained the definitions of first and second degree murder and manslaughter, the definition of malice; the statement that it is the prosecution's job to prove guilt; that the defendant is presumed innocent until proven guilty, etc. The instructions were very general in determining if the defendant was guilty. However, in determining if the defendant was not guilty, the Court stated:

> *...that it is your sworn duty to consider the testimony of the defendant fairly and impartially, and if there is any reasonable doubt as to whether the shooting resulted from accident, your verdict must be "not guilty".*

The Court instructed the jurors that the defendant:

> *...had a legal right to possess and carry the shotgun introduced into evidence, and the*

defendant had a further legal right to have said shotgun loaded.

The instructions became explicit:

> *The Court instructs you that the defendant in this case, at the time of the commission of the alleged offense, had a right to be let alone and that the deceased had no right to take pictures of the defendant over his protest. The defendant had a right to earn his living by receiving compensation for pictures of himself and in so doing he was violating no law.*
>
> *You are further instructed that the defendant had the same right to travel upon the highways of this state with his cart and donkeys as do persons traveling by motor vehicles—and in so traveling he was violating no law and he had a right to be let alone.*
>
> *If you find from the evidence that the deceased intended to take pictures of the defendant without his consent, and attempted to do so, you are instructed that the defendant had a right to object and to use all reasonable means to prevent a violation of his right of privacy and of his property rights in and to the peculiar appearance of himself, his cart and donkeys...*" [the following was added in pencil]... *" but he had, of course, no right, intentionally to take human life, in so doing.*

In determining whether the means intended to be used by the defendant, at the time of the tragedy involved, were reasonable, you are instructed that you should consider the circumstances surrounding the transaction, the respective ages of the defendant and deceased, the fact, (if you find it to be a fact) of the helplessness of the defendant under the circumstances, and you should view the transaction in the light of the excitement under which you find the defendant was laboring to protect his rights, if you so find.

Situations sometime arise in a man's life in which he cannot be held to the same degree of care and prudence as he would ordinarily exercise. In such situations his conduct must be judged in the light of the difficulties under which he was laboring at the time.

The instructions were a little biased, especially by today's standards. Could it be that it was the court's attempt at swaying the jury towards a not guilty verdict?

The jurors were further instructed to not consider the plea of insanity. Whether or not the defendant was sane at the time of the murder was not the issue.

The judge instructed that the jurors were not to infer from discussions he had had with the attorneys, by his attitudes or other statements he made during the trial that he had expressed any opinion about the facts.

The jurors were then led to the third floor of the courthouse to deliberate, and Pete was taken to the county garage so he could inspect his cart. He ran his hand lovingly around its wheels as he confidently posed for newspaper photographers. "The jury will find me not guilty." He was sure of it.

The Verdict

After 50 minutes of deliberation, the defendant and attorneys were summoned to return to the courtroom. It was July 2, nearly four months since the fatal shooting. The verdict was handed to the court clerk to read. "Not Guilty!" The courtroom broke into applause that could be heard spilling out the courthouse and into the street. Pete sobbed in relief, as did some of the jurors.

News of the trial, and especially of the verdict, hit newspapers and radios from coast to coast. The media had covered the spectacular story about how an old man who lived in the mountains and traveled throughout California with his burros had killed a man for simply taking his picture. People all over the country had followed the story and were anxiously awaiting the verdict. A young reporter living in Great Falls, Montana, also followed the story. His name was George Heintz, my father.

While people across the country were stunned at the verdict, the attorney's family was enraged. How could someone be acquitted of murder when there were no less than three witnesses to the shooting?

Pete had his supporters though. He had touched the hearts of many with his dirt-poor appearance and emotional testimony. Each day, the courtroom was packed with people eager to get a glimpse of the bearded old man. The three young defense attorneys, Foley, Menard, and Kirby, took a special liking to their client, even calling him "dad." At least one of the jurors was outwardly sympathetic toward Pete; as she walked past him, she pressed a $5 bill into his hand.

The Assistant District Attorney Charles McDonnell's performance in the courtroom was weak, at best, in trying to prove a case against Pete. Interestingly, in December of 1936, five months after the trial, McDonnell resigned his position. Who would be his successor? It was none other than Napoleon J. Menard, one of Pete's own defense attorneys!

Ladies pose with Pete and his burros, most likely in front of
the Appeal-Democrat Newspaper in Marysville, CA

Chapter 9

After the Trial

After he was released from custody, Pete stepped outside the courthouse, his eyes squinting at the bright sunlight. For 69 days he had been in a dinky, gloomy cage that had kept him away from his mountains, earth and sunlit sky. The laws of society separated him from his best friends, his three burros: Jimmy, Trixy and Doc. He missed his freedom to roam through his beloved mountains and streams with his burros. His missed the solitude of the wide-open space away from the city's cement. He missed the call of the ore: *Gold*!

His attorneys took his arms and assisted him to their car. They drove him to Sacramento where his friends, Dr. and Mrs. Durfee, met him. On their way to Auburn, they stopped in Roseville [both in Placer County], just in time for the town's annual Fourth of July celebration. To Pete's astonishment, the crowds welcomed him with a warm reception. People cheered and applauded him as he timidly took the microphone in his hands and addressed the crowds.

"Thank you all for your support these past two months. They were hard months. Now I must rest." Then he handed the microphone back to the emcee. Many people in Placer County had contributed their nickels and dimes towards his defense, and Pete was grateful.

The trio arrived in Auburn shortly before 5 o'clock p.m., where numerous informal receptions awaited Pete throughout the town. Again, Pete made his way among the crowds to thank the people for their support. But, it was his burros that he missed the most and he was anxious to see them again.

Later that evening, Pete, along with Dr. Durfee, slipped away, and Dr. Durfee took him to see his burros. They were corralled on the Terry ranch in the Rock Creek District, just a couple of miles from the Durfee ranch. Pete, eyes brimming with tears of joy at seeing his faithful friends, nuzzled the burros and gave them pieces of candy. Doc, especially, was happy to see his master. He placed his front feet up on Pete's chest in greeting, nearly knocking him down. Doc liked his beer, so the two of them shared a bottle that night in celebration, much like the following picture:

Pete sharing a bottle of beer with Doc

It had been an emotional day, and Pete was exhausted. They headed to the Durfee ranch where Pete could finally lay his head down. He slept soundly for the first time in more than two months.

He awoke at sunrise to the intense smell of bacon frying and coffee brewing. Mrs. Durfee, a matronly woman who liked to cook, was in the kitchen fixing a breakfast of bacon and eggs, potatoes and toast. The smell of breakfast lured him into the kitchen, where he sat down to the best meal he'd had in quite some time. He was thankful for the meal, yet was hoping to rest more. But Dr. Durfee hurried him along. Pete was to be the guest-of-honor at the Georgetown and Grass Valley Independence Day celebrations.

Pete and Dr. Durfee climbed into the doctor's truck and headed up the hill to Georgetown then over to Grass Valley. The two men walked among the crowds of families enjoying picnics on the park's lawns at both locations. Pete again thanked people for their support during the past couple of months. Some folks asked him about the trial, but he shied away from those discussions. He just wanted to forget it ever happened. "I knew the truth would come out—it had to," he said. "Now I must go away to my mountains."

The scene was similar in both Georgetown and Grass Valley. Children played baseball, tag, and hide-and-go-seek in the summer's warm afternoon. Dogs barked as they chased after rubber balls their owners threw to them. Soon the evening would arrive with its cooler air, and the sky would darken. People anxiously awaited the evening's fireworks.

But not Pete. He'd had enough of the crowds. By late afternoon, he and Dr. Durfee had returned to the ranch. Now that the celebrations were over, he could settle in, fatten up on some of Mrs. Durfee's good cooking, and get some much-needed rest before heading for his mountains.

He spent most of his days at the ranch writing, but the best part of each day was the early evenings. After the warm sunshine went down over the Sierra foothills, and Dr.

Durfee had returned from his day's work, he drove Pete out to the Terry ranch for a much-anticipated visit with his burros.

Trixy, Jimmy and Doc came running at the sight of their master, who always had a piece of candy for them. Pete hugged and petted his burros while talking to them and promising that they would leave soon for their mountains.

Letter from a Friend

While recuperating at the Durfee's ranch, Pete received a kind letter from a friend. He must have been touched by the friend's words, for he carried the letter with him in the old black purse for nearly the rest of his life. On July 11, 1936, Alvin McCreary wrote:

Dear "Dad":

I know you won't remember my name, but I think you'll remember me all right when I recall the night I had the heart attack and you saved my life in that awful place. I certainly shall never forget the experience; neither will I ever forget your kindness to me.

You remember the next day I left and went to a Sanitarium. I was there a week. And while I got along fairly well physically, the constant thinking, thinking about the whole thing was holding me back and I couldn't get any sleep. I just couldn't get over thinking about the worry I was causing my family, my sister and my friends to say nothing of losing my job away out here 3000 miles from home. After a week of it the doctor let me come back here at the above hotel where he thought I would be better off. I've been here ever since taking in "movies" and lying around trying to get my mind off it. Then yesterday the

BIG NEWS came. I got a wire from my co. saying, "all is forgiven and when would I be able to start for Seattle, Wash. to start to work again." Well, you can imagine my feelings. I was 100% better immediately and wired right back that I was ready to go at once, but the dr. wanted me to wait till Monday or Tuesday.

So I'm going to leave not later than Tues. I'm still a little "shaky" and that's the reason I'm writing with a pencil. But as soon as I get one day's work in I'll be all right.

I've told you all about myself, now let's talk about you. While I was in the Sanitarium, I read every paper I could get hold of about your trial, also listened to all radio news flashes. I was listening to the radio when the news came that you were acquitted. And honestly I can't begin to describe how happy I was. It did me more good than all the medicine I had taken. And I tell you I wasn't the only one that was happy at the San. I had told them about meeting you and all about you.

Now I sincerely hope you are rested up and feeling fine again. It was an awful ordeal, I know and I shouldn't even mention my trouble in comparison. But I surely am glad we are both getting a new start. I know it's been a wonderful lesson for me. And I feel sorry for the boys that are still back there in that awful place.

I know I'll be glad to get out of this town and try to forget. And I know you were too.

I meant to write you long before this and wanted to see you before you left, but they wouldn't let me out and I was too shaky to write. Now I would be mighty glad to hear from you sometime and let me know how you are. You can write me care of this hotel and they will forward it to me. I won't know my address in Seattle till I get there.

So here's hoping you have the best of luck in all your travels or anything you do. And thanks again for the nice things you did for me.

Sincerely your friend,

Alvin McCreary
El Camino Hotel
San Jose, Calif.

(139 W. Santa Clara St., San Jose)

The "awful place" that McCreary refers to could be a mine that he and Pete had worked in when McCreary had a heart attack. Who could forget someone who saved your life? The trial brought Pete to the forefront, so his friend decided to write him to offer his thanks and to reestablish their relationship.

Pete stuffed the letter inside the black purse, intending to write the man, when he finally got his cart back from San Jose. He and his burros were ready to move on and to be free again. He said his good-byes to the Durfee's while hitching his burros to the cart. Slowly, they pulled away and headed toward the mountains ahead.

Chapter 10

Return to Freedom

Freedom! Ah, the sweet sound of Freedom! Pete was now free to travel the roads to his mountains and sky, to be near his God. No more iron bars to hold him. He wanted only to be held tightly by his outdoors, to work the earth, to sleep, and to make hotcakes for his beloved burros.

He had been on the road a couple of days when he rounded a bend near a portion of the American River where men and women were swimming. The women, in their brief bathing suits, came running up to Pete to offer their greetings. The burros became skittish.

"Why are those donkeys acting like that?" one of the women asked.

"They are not used to seeing such brief garments with so much skin showing," he explained. "Perhaps by 1940 they will no longer be afraid of your swimming suits."

The women giggled and skipped back to their swimming hole.

Pete moved on, traveling deeper into the mountains. He met no one else along the way, and that was fine with him. He was anxious to find a miner's cabin where he could stay a while and search for gold.

He was so happy to be traveling again with his burros. They were his only companions. With them, he shared his food and his life. When there was money for an extravagant meal, he shared it with them. Sure, he loved children and a few good men that he met along the way, but he preferred his burros to all of them. They talked to him as he talked to them. They worked as a team with a keen understanding of each other.

In the following story Pete describes this understanding and connection with his burros:

Animal Life and Their Reason Power
Peter Voiss

Larks bathing in the mountain springs.
Nature's life—of freedom sings.

A short description of animals' reasoning power as I observed it. A true story of different animals, but especially of the writer's donkeys. Nature lovers will not find it dull and enjoy to read these adventures.

Nature's wilds, I adore—freedom, where no right or wrong.
Laws and culture's sins, I scorn.
Unbridled wilds—to you my song.

All animals select their food, the donkey, as an exception never drinks bad water; if he refused it there is something wrong. A man could not try to drink. Very very seldom gets sick and when hurt, cures his own wounds with certain clay. A dog laps his wound. Some animals are helpless in this regard. Indians I remember use clay on top of the wounds.
You take dogs understand mankind. The best they learn quicker with exception of the elephant, the most trustful friend in life. All animals are aware and watchful of danger and they reason according to their treatment.

Biber ants are great builders of their houses, surprising how animals reason for winter shelter food. Some store their food for bad cold weather.

As a general instinct they are all good mothers and watch and take care of their offspring and see to it that they get sufficient food for their development. They learn them to eat certain food in order that the capacity of nursing is in the decline.

But they cannot talk to humans, but they are in danger in want of food. They soon let you know and bark, brae, or holler to obtain their needs.

As I had 3 donkeys braying, there was something wrong either tangled in rope, or one loose and the others warned me. I had dog; he barked when he wanted to come in or out. Horses and donkeys always brae by the sight of their master.

If a person takes time it can train any animal. As the first rule he must feed them right, never scare or threat or punish them. The friendship you offer an animal, slowly it will accept. Some animals reason quicker as others.

On my prospect travels I came across a tree squirrel with cat's head. It was awful shy, so I set some milk out and canned fish, as I came back it was eating hardly a bite by the sight of me runned off. I keep on feeding in 4 weeks it was on my lap. It was an interbreed of a housecat. Then it started to follow me every step. As it got colder it like to lay along the stove. Before I had a lot of mice and packrats. She kept on hunting them.

As I went away I did not like to take it along. First my donkeys did not like it. Then too I think freedom, the most highest ideal of nature, is the best for this kind animal. I left food for all winter and a good cabin to sneak in.

I came back in the spring. My friend was gone. I felt kind sorry. All I hope that it is well. Many many times bear or deer came to eat my garbage but I never bothered them, but I enjoyed them very much. I had a lost fawn for 3 months feed her milk with the bottle and other food. But one day it left and a month afterwards came for a brief visit. I could not touch it anymore. It went back to primitive life.

All animals like to be patted if they reason that you do not hurt them. I had bullcalf nobody could touch, little by little I make friend to me. Today if it sees me it comes right up to me.

All animals esteem the person who feeds them and does right to them.

I saw animals who bit, kicked and jumped up in the air. I never saw one who did not reason never hurt a person who done right to them. All animals like partnershp if they have not, they adopt one. Dogs will adopt nearly any animal and never hurt. Instead they will protect them. It seems hard to them if they get parted. They do not easy forget. Horses—donkeys—if they worked as teams cannot be worked for a long time; single, they like to go and play together. Mother animals are liable to adopt other kind young animal and raise it, furnish food to them. Till today I cannot understand the reason why they feel that way to help others besides their own. Even these cases are often proved by wild animals like wolves do it.

All like sugar, except cats like fish. The most sugar is great in training certain animals they know why they reason.

A dog is the greatest true friend to humans, even if their master or Mrs. dies, the dog will watch them and mourn a long long time. Their faithfulness is of such an extent that they even fight those who try to take charge of their master.

I came after long studying animal life that they have a reason power—it works very slow—and there is always understanding between partners (animals) to reason to give signs of joy or danger by braying, hollering, etc., and assist each other in danger. If possible, to encourage each other. Many a time I noticed that I drove a team up hill one animal encourages the other, that soon would the top be reached. Many times I came about 5 miles from where they been for months. I did not drive them just to see what they do. They runned, shook their heads and on a branch road turned and came up to ranch without touching the lines. After 2 years they never forgot they had no map, but they know. But they been farther than 600 miles and did not forget.

For the desert where no water was available for 30-40 miles ants living even I saw often jackrabbits, coyotes, etc., but very lean, they seem to make a living what little vegetation there was. My donkeys make always out, they find a little here and underneath the sagebrush or cactus, they eat cactus. I took the dorns off and sliced it. Still I fed them a little grain but in the morning they never forgot their hotcakes. I make each one a big hotcake. Humans who enjoy nature and the wild know that all my writing is correct.

I do not believe Darwin's writings that humans are descended of animals, but it is proved many times that humans walked on hands and feet in primitive times. The development of his brain did make humans superior to animals, and found use for animals, for his ends in every possible way to bring man comfort in his life.

Pete was feeling rather light hearted when he wrote the following poem about a bar of soap.

Ivory Soap

Peter Voiss

The great invention, I hope you get the
pension
It is so real, that everybody likes to steal
It curls the hair, the bald heads are not in
despair
Mondays see the ladies smile, the laundry is
just right
Ivory soap the great dope, it makes the
colored white
Mary would not tell Johnny to behave
For Ivory soap now he can get a shave
If you put a tire on, oh it's swell
It has a scent but there is no smell
It swims along, never drowns

They mark the cake where it breaks in half
So if they swipe it you laugh
You got still the Ivory left
Hotel put it on a chain
Say that stunt is not in vain
If you come on Heaven's door
Peter may say No—you sin
Just tell him Ivory soap
And he let you in
And oh along the roads in big signs
Ivory soap, hot dogs in big lines

See my whiskers are so bright
It's Ivory soap what a delight
The burros are so clean and nice
Ivory soap gets the first prize

It cleans the gear and the car
The rooster and the hen
The pot and the pan
The donkey and the monkey

It's fine for bath or shampoo
Listen I tell you something new
Surely it makes the flu skiddoo
If you eat it cold
You never feel old

Ivory soap, that's the dope
Just hear the radio, but what a mess
Premiums Ivory soap and gas
For in Ivory soap 3 cheers
Success a 1000 years

People called him "Old Man of the Mountains," a fitting description. It was in his soft and warm mountains that he was able to feel whole again. It was in nature's solitude that he was able to work hard during the day and to rest at night. He played with his burros, and they worked hard along with their master. After a few weeks, Pete was ready to resume his wanderings.

Pete with his burros

Chapter 11

The Accident

Pete had overcome one ordeal, but another wasn't far behind. He headed west again, traveling just on the outskirts of Sacramento, through Vallejo and Martinez. He and his rig drove slowly into Martinez at dusk one October evening in 1936. He was deep in thought and minding his own business when suddenly he heard the roar of a truck come up behind him. Before he could pull to the side, it plowed into the rear of the cart. The cart broke apart easily and looked as if toothpicks had been scattered across the road. Pete fell to the ground with one of the wheels on top of him. Somehow the frightened burros managed to stay tied together and did not stray far.

The driver of the truck admittedly was driving recklessly when he hit the cart team. Of course, he wasn't injured, and his heavy company truck only had a small dent in it. After answering questions from the policeman, he was able to go home to his family.

Not so for Pete. The accident landed him in the local hospital and his burros in the pound. The nurses cleaned the guy up a bit, but he adamantly refused their request to cut his beard. That was taking this cleanliness thing a bit too far, in Pete's way of thinking. His beard was part of his identity; no one was about to cut it off! After mending for a few days in the hospital, he convinced the doctors to release him. Whether he was medically ready to be released, or because he was just too feisty to keep within the confines of the institution, the doctors agreed to let him go.

With the help of some friends, Pete was able to assemble another two-wheeled cart. He bailed his burros out of the pound, and he, Jimmy, Trixy and Doc were happily on the road again. He and the burros were so shaken by the accident, that one evening while resting far away at the foot of a mountain, Pete wrote this poem to his burros:

Promise to Donkeys After the Accident
Peter Voiss

I take you back to hills and meadows lawn
Away, away of thundering motor's pressure
Where you can play with bark, doe and fawn
Where you enjoy freedom's life with pleasure.

Far away...where we live in peace
Larks bathing in the mountain springs
Where daddy digs gold in ease
And nature's life, of freedom sings.
No noisy kids make you run
No bridle hurt, no saddle press your back
Enjoy hotcakes by rising sun
Jump, roll, no halter shave your neck.

Through deserts, hills, trained your feet
Proud carried Jesus through Jesus alien's street
Ye faithful souls off and bolt
We never part for a ton of gold.

After a couple of painful months, in December, Pete decided to come back into Martinez where he filed a $7,000 lawsuit against a Martinez trucking firm and the driver. He asked $5,000 in general damages, $1,000 for destruction of the cart, $500 because his burros "were frightened and became jittery", and $5 a day for the time he was unable to "work" posing for photographs. He claimed his right leg was partially paralyzed and he suffered frequent headaches because of the accident.

As it turned out, the driver of the truck got away with a $100 fine for reckless driving. Pete decided to drop the suit. The law just confounded him and he didn't want to hang around the city for another trial. He preferred to keep right on wandering.

Months later, in August of 1937, Pete decided he wanted his ancient shotgun back. After the accident the previous year, all of his equipment had been scattered across the road, including the shotgun. Naturally, the sheriff confiscated the gun and had it in his safekeeping. This was the same shotgun that was used to take a life the year before; however, it had been returned to Pete after the trial with the pin removed. So now Pete wanted it back. He needed it to complete the look of an old prospector, or so he said, as the sheriff handed him his gun.

Woman shaking hands with Doc

Chapter 12

Mad as a Hatter

In the fall of 1937 Pete was posing for pictures in Merced. It had been more than a year since he'd been accused and acquitted of murder, and still he had no tolerance for people who insisted on trying to take his picture without paying him. Since the trial he felt a little bolder. He knew he had a right to protect his home; he knew he had a right to protect his income. So when a young woman tried to take his picture, he ran after her and grabbed her hair. She ran away and got into her car, leaving him with her hat and a fist full of hair. "Dumm kopf! [stupid head] Pay me or leave me be!" he grumbled to himself as he stomped on the hat and walked off.

Pete all dressed up

Chapter 13

Women and the Road

Pete knew that a prospector's life was no life to share with a woman. He felt a woman deserved to be around beautiful things and should not have to live in filthy mining camps or suffer hardships of living in the mountains away from civilization. He never married.

Although he was perfectly content to share his life with his burros and did not consider himself a lonely man, there were times when he craved the company of a woman. Among his belongings was a large photograph of a beautiful woman. The only identification was "Aviatrix from Sacramento" written on the back of the picture.

He did have several liaisons with women and wrote about some:

The Unsuccessful Buggy Ride
Peter Voiss

Long years ago I frequented with a girl of a friend of me. This lady was a widow and had a family of three girls and one boy. I know Irene quite well and I took her out in a buggy ride. I rented a buggy and horse for $3.00. She enjoyed it very much. We did drink some soda pop and went out in the country. We stop underneath a big tree. She admired the country but I admired her the most. I wanted to love her. I guess I was too hot and excited; she jumped up and went towards home. I went to the buggy and hit the old horse up to catch up with her. As I did she sternly refuse to ride. She walked and I rode to the barn to *bring the horse back, then went to her home. Her mother laughed out loud at me, "That suits you right. Irene had told me about your failure, and I would have done the same thing."*

I told Irene I would take more time to heat you up first. She shaked her head and smiled. We still were friends but I did not succeed.

The Dream Baby

Peter Voiss

Years ago I make a 70 feet deep well for X. I done it several times several periodic jobs for the party. I was very well acquainted say good friends and his wife was too, sometimes very familiar.

About 6 months later I came back to see the X and the Mrs. X showed me her baby boy and told me if it was not looking like X? X told her it looked like the neighbor and had no use for the kid.... Or, she said to me, does it look like you?

For heaven sake, I done it only once. You will not have me shot for that, besides it was 6 months ago. I could not even put the ears on, I said to her. I said then to her, maybe it is dream baby, that you dreamed about the neighbor as you was in contact with your husband. (She runned over to the neighbor, a bachelor, always make cakes and pies for him).

Anyway, the X been fighting always, so one day she got a divorce and ½ of the land. And today she is married to the neighbor. Whenever X gets drunk he marched along the fence with a gun on shoulder, several times the pair had him arrested, but he does it again when drunk.

Who is to blame?

Pete gets a little sugar from Doc

Chapter 14

New Baby and the Fair

While traversing through the hills of Mariposa County in the spring of 1938, Pete caught a young wild burro that he named LaMae. He claimed to have trained her in four days and that she was the smartest of the bunch. If you held your hand out to her, she would shake hands, for a price. But be careful, when her master said, "Kick!," she kicked! She also liked to have a beer and to smoke a good cigar. Pete taught his burros well!

On Labor Day the following September, an old, bearded man wearing a hat and tattered clothes came into Turlock on his burro when a car hit and killed him. When they learned that the victim was Peter Voiss, the old prospector who had been acquitted of murder two years before, the community was shocked. He was buried without fanfare or funeral, yet the townspeople mourned his death. When Pete surfaced a couple of months later, he denied he was dead! It turned out that the victim had been a look-alike and the real Pete was alive and well.

Pete wandered around Northern California for a few months, when, in late 1938, he was spotted traveling through Vallejo on his way to San Francisco with his three older burros and his new baby burro. He told folks he had a business meeting to discuss picture-taking at the World's Fair when it opened the following February.

On his way to San Francisco, Pete found himself in trouble with the law once again. While traveling through Palo Alto in January 1939, Pete noticed a man standing on the running board of his car with a camera pointing at him and his strange rig. Angry that someone else was about to take his picture without his permission, he came after the man with a club. The two men got into a scuffle and bystanders had to pull them apart.

Someone called the sheriff and Pete was jailed, with his burros locked up at the pound again. Pete pled not guilty to the assault charge and was held on $50 bail. When word reached his friend and benefactor, Dr. Durfee, he came to his rescue and bailed Pete and his burros out of jail, giving the old man another chance.

Pete was anxious to be on his way and to talk to the businessman about the upcoming World's Fair.

Everyone was eager with anticipation for opening day of the Golden Gate International Exposition; it was to be the first big event held on San Francisco's newly completed Treasure Island. The Depression was coming to a close and San Francisco had recently completed two new bridges: The San Francisco-Oakland Bridge (as it was originally called) and the Golden Gate Bridge. It was a time for celebration and Pete was looking forward to being a part of it. He knew there was money to be made with all of those tourists.

The businessman thought Pete would be a good draw for the fair, as well as for California. Pete was the essence of California's Gold Rush days, with his straggly appearance and his cart and burros. Placed out by the water's edge on Treasure Island, Pete and his burros posed for picture after picture. It was LaMae's first time at having her picture taken, and she didn't mind hamming it up a bit for the photographer. Jimmy wore blinders; he was afraid of the water, according to Pete.

Pete and his burros advertising the World's Fair

The negatives of these pictures and more were found inside the black purse. The Golden Gate Bridge can be seen in the background of one of the pictures. Pete had several of his pictures copyrighted, as evidenced by cards received from the Copyright office acknowledging receipt of the photos.

Pete had several of his pictures made into postcards and began selling them throughout the duration of the fair, with the first run of the fair ending in October 1939. The old guy made a goodly sum of money during that time as he roamed the fairgrounds. Children came up to him and he let them ride his donkeys; he posed for pictures with some of the fairgoers; and LaMae did her tricks, all in the name of money. We know for sure that Pete made a buck from a young reporter who would later stumble across his belongings in an old mine.

Pete liked the idea of having his pictures put on the backs of postcards, so with some of the money he made from the fair, he bought a Brownie camera for $1.00 and began having his friends take his pictures as he came through town. He began advertising his postcards on his wagon: "Pictures For Sale—14 kinds," or "We Sell Pictures to Live." Occasionally he even sold a poem.

Pete with burros Trixy, Jimmy, and Doc. LaMae is next to Pete,
advertising the World's Fair

More posing by the water's edge

Posing with new baby burro, LaMae

Pete playing with LaMae

Pete and LaMae

Pete and his burros relaxing after pictures advertising the World's Fair

Chapter 15

War Years

World War II dominated the first half of the 1940s, and the Great Depression ended due to war production. It was the era of the Big Bands and Rosie the Riveter as women joined the work force in positions vacated by our servicemen. Food and gas rationing affected people's lives, ice cream was hard to find; and the production of women's nylons ended.

Pete hung around the San Francisco area throughout the early 1940s. Webb's Photo Supply Store located at 66 South 1st Street in San Jose developed his film and mounted the photographs on postcards from 1938 to, at least, 1941. Pete had a running account with this store, which he always kept current. In August of 1939, Pete was using the address of 2898 Sloat Boulevard in San Francisco, and by March of 1941 his address was at 2799 Taylor Street in San Francisco.

The address on Taylor Street was the residence of his good friend Evelyn Montijo Evans, with whom he stayed when she and her first husband lived in Alameda in 1910. Her husband William had passed away some years before and she had remarried, this time to Thomas Evans. The couple moved to San Francisco where he was a fisherman and she was a waitress with the Neptune Fish Grotto at 2737 Taylor Street, just down the street from their residence. The restaurant opened in 1936 and was famous for its chioppino, fried crab legs, abalone, deviled crabs, and charcoal broiled fish.

Wednesday, February 5th, 1941

NEPTUNE
FISH GROTTO

Glass of Red or White Wine, 10c

FRESH GOLDEN BANTAM CORN ON COB 20
Fried Egg Plant 20   Fresh Spinach 15

HALF CRACKED CRAB 40; WHOLE CRAB 80

CHOWDERS

GENUINE BOSTON CLAM CHOWDER (creamy) 15
CONEY ISLAND CLAM CHOWDER (with tomatoes) 15
PURE CLAM BROTH IN CUP 15

TODAY'S SPECIALTIES
BROILED HALF LOBSTER 80; WHOLE BABY LOBSTER 1.00

BROILED TURBOT WITH LEMON BUTTER 50
CRAB LEGS AND PRAWNS A LA CREOLE EN CASSEROLE .. 65
FRIED EASTERN SCALLOPS, LOUIE SAUCE 60
BODEGA BAY BONELESS SMELTS, MEUNIERE 50
BARRACUDA CHIOPPINO WITH CRAB AND RICE 65

COMBINATION SEA FOOD PLATE A LA "CHEF" 75c

SUGGESTIONS

Spaghetti with Crab Meat, Fisherman Style 50
Broiled Fresh Mackerel, Parsley Butter 40
Boiled Alaska Cod with Steamed Potatoes 60
Fresh Crab Salad .... 50; a la Louie 60
Deviled Crab Meat, Baked in Shell 60
Fried Fresh Eastern Scallops, Tartar Sauce 60
Broiled Salmon Steak, Parsley Butter 50
Fresh Crab or Shrimp a la Creole en Casserole 60
Fried Boneless Smelts with Parsley Butter 40
Filet of English Sole, Tartar Sauce 40
Half Dozen Eastern Oysters, Fried 50
Olympia Oysters, Hangtown Fry 70
Fried Fresh Crab Legs, Butter Sauce 60

BROILED BROOK TROUT Butter Sauce — 75c —	FRIED FROG LEGS Meuniere or Butter Sauce — 85c —

OYSTER LOAVES, SALADS, CHOWDERS, etc., Put Up To Take Home

Surely, Pete and his burros were eating well during this time. When he came into the cities, he spent his nights camped on the outskirts away from people, coming into town during the day to sell his pictures. He needed an address for Webb's Photo Supply Store to send his completed postcard pictures to him. Friends in the cities were glad to let him use their addresses. He met kind people along the way, some taking him in for the night so he could bathe, eat a hot meal, and leave with some clean clothes. These kind folks usually sent him on his way with some food to tide him over for a few days.

One of the respondents to my father's request for information about Pete was Alta May Crawford. She had traveled to San Francisco in December 1940 to visit her friend, and Pete's, Evelyn Evans. It was at this time that she met Pete when the two women took some fruit out to him. She described him as a kindly, old gentleman, but he didn't like people barging in on him.

After the introductions, and a little small talk, the women started on their way, but Pete called out to Alta May: "Mrs. Crawford, come back here. Ev, I'll talk to you later."

Alta May turned back and returned to Pete. "Yes?"

"I've got this paper. I need you to sign," he told her. "It's typed up real pretty. I'll sign my name, then you sign here, " as he pointed to the spot on the paper.

Alta May did as she was asked, oblivious to the purpose of the paper she'd signed. After signing her name without question, Pete grumbled his thanks and she joined her friend inside the house.

Pete was nearly 80 years old. He knew it wouldn't be long before his time on earth would end, and he wanted to dispose of his belongings. Inside the black purse was this bill of sale:

Bill of Sale (Tax paid)

I sell all my property 4, burros, names, Jimmy, LaMae, Trixy, Doc,cart, and all personal possessions, and belongings, to Mrs. Evelyn M. Evans of San Francisco, for one dollar in U.S. coin.

Peter Voiss

Dated: December 21, 1940
San Francisco, California

(signed)
Witness: Alta May Crawford
524 Westminster Street
Fresno, Calif.

Pete had known Evelyn Evans a long time and he knew he could trust her to care for his family of burros. His friends, the Durfee's, had departed the Auburn area for Southern California, so it was necessary that he find someone else to care for his burros.

Despite his intentions to have Mrs. Evans be the caretaker, the arrangement was short lived. Mrs. Evans suddenly died just a few months later. Undaunted, Pete continued to find someone to take his burros in the event he passed away.

Chapter 16

End of the Trail

Pete's wanderings began to slow during the 1940s. He was in his eighth decade by now and his body and mind were becoming increasingly feeble. By the fall of 1941, he'd had enough of city life and was anxious to return to his mountains. He and his burros left San Francisco, heading into the mountains. He found a cabin to shelter him from the harsh mountain elements; a place he could use while he wrote his stories with the warmth of the fireplace. His furry friends woke him early in the mornings, ready for their hotcakes. If the burros were good, he might bring them inside the cabin for their treat, as long as they didn't get too frisky and cause a calamity.

Springtime came and he sifted a little in the streams while looking for flakes of gold. With little success, he knew it was time to return to the city where tourists would buy his pictures so he could provide for himself. He rounded up his burros, hitched them up and came down out of the mountains and gulches. As he headed down the hills towards Stockton, he stopped for a while in the old mining town of Jenny Lind. He knew about an old mineshaft that he had frequented in the past, so it was there that he camped and rested.

His mind was failing, so perhaps he forgot about the black purse which he had tied to the mine's beam before heading back to civilization. Although Pete continued his wanderings over the next two years, he never returned to the mine in Jenny Lind. The old purse hung alone in the dark damp mine for many years, waiting to be found.

Pete left behind a part of his life in that old black purse: his pictures and their negatives, his stories, the poem he had written as a young man in Germany that landed him in the fortress. Inside the purse was a photo of Thomas Clements, the founder of Clements, California. On the back is written "Miss M. Clements" with a San Jose address. [This is probably Thomas' daughter Margaret Clements.] Pete left behind handmade Christmas cards with photographs of children that families had sent him, pictures of prospectors torn from magazines, and of course, the pencil stub he had used to write his stories.

By 1944, Pete had given up his wanderings and returned to Alameda County to stay. His cart was still his castle as he and his burros stuck close to the towns in and near Alameda. His health was failing, and he felt ill much of the time. He moved around somewhat, but usually stayed put at the edge of town. He continued to be a curiosity to city dwellers. Some just stared. Others would sneak up close and hand him some food, then run away. The food he was given kept him going, along with the generosity of the butcher who occasionally gave him a slab of meat to eat. Of course, he gladly shared it with his burros. A friendship developed each time the butcher came by with the meat and chatted with him.

By August of 1946, Pete and his rig were camping out in a field in Oakland. Nearby construction workers walked out to him every morning to offer him a cup of coffee from their thermoses and to ask how he was getting along. When they noticed that he was beginning to stumble and fall, they became concerned. One of the workers called an ambulance. When the ambulance arrived, the first-aid team found the old man, unconscious, lying on the ground beside his cart. As the thin, gravely ill prospector was carefully lifted onto a gurney, his burros looked on, clearly worried about their master. Pete was taken to nearby Highland Hospital for emergency care. His burros were taken, once again, to the city pound.

Pete was given a bath, probably the first in several years, and put in a bed between clean sheets. Doctors ran tests and determined he had both a heart ailment and liver cirrhosis. Once stabilized, he was transferred to Fairmont Hospital in San Leandro, ten miles away. For the next five weeks needles poked and fingers prodded the old man; he was completely at the mercy of others to care for him as he slipped in and out of consciousness.

News about his illness reached the butcher, and on September 13, 1946, his friend paid him a visit and assured Pete that he would take good care of his burros. Pete smiled weakly, then closed his eyes for the last time as he left this world for the gold mine in the sky.

Following his death, the butcher produced a handwritten will in which Pete had given him custody of his burros. He presented it to the Pound Master, then took the burros to his ranch in San Ramon. They were pastured there until their deaths.

Pete's only known relative, a nephew who lived in Portland, Oregon, was notified of his uncle's death. He was asked to claim the body and make funeral arrangements, but when he didn't show, locals took over. A number of people who had seen the old man camping out and perhaps had said a word or two to him, got together and provided for a funeral. They thought it was only proper that the hermit, who had been a part of California's rich gold heritage, should have a funeral of beauty and respect.

Pete was cremated, and his ashes were scattered among his burros in their new pasture. He was finally at one with Mother Earth. The cart was erected on railroad ties in the pasture as a tribute to the old man of the mountains who had provided such a colorful part of California's history.

Sadly I Leave You
Peter Voiss

When happy days come to an end
And I go to the bigger gold fields
It's faraway around the bend
Hardships and life abound with gilt.

On Lord's call we smile of the past
When they press my eyelids down
There is deep sorrow in my heart
That I can't take ye faithful soul along.

Chapter 17

On Reflection

As I traveled the route between Stockton and San Jose, I thought about Pete making the same trip in the 1930s and 1940s with his cart and burros. He would surely think Interstates 205, 580 and 680 were raceways with drivers eager to see who could get to San Jose first. Today, this trip takes less than 90 minutes. In Pete's day, the same trip took him and his burros a good four days!

If Pete were out competing with big SUVs, semi and tanker trucks, motor homes, motorcycles and other modern vehicles, whizzing by at 70 miles an hour, the poor guy and his burros would be terrified. The team would either be run off the road into the ravines near Altamont Pass or his spectacle would create numerous accidents. More likely, he and his burros would be killed in short order.

I felt drawn to visit the area where the shooting occurred alongside the Monterey Highway. Portions of the highway outside Morgan Hill appear to be suspended in time, with the exception of the concrete median that separates its more modern four lanes. Cherry orchards dress the side of the road much as they did in 1936. Franklin Darcey, a successful attorney, and Pete, a crusty, old gold prospector, traveled this 22-mile stretch of road between Morgan Hill and San Jose many times for different reasons. I couldn't help but feel their presence as I, too, traveled this same stretch of road.

Finally, I continued on to San Ramon. The ranch where Pete's ashes were scattered among his burros is long gone, replaced with Interstate 580 where cars zoom by the town without a thought to what happened here many years ago.

Much has changed since the old prospector wandered in and around these cities. Mountains and rolling hills surround the San Francisco Bay Area, many now dotted with housing developments. Pete rested in these same mountains when he visited the cities, a perfect escape from the concrete below.

In 1936, it may have been legal to mix cars with a cart and burros on the open roads, but in today's world, Pete surely would have been arrested or taken off the road and put into a homeless shelter or left to camp beneath a bridge. His beloved burros would be taken from him.

There are more laws today than in Pete's time. Certainly, carrying a loaded gun in your vehicle would be one of them that would get Pete some attention from the law. Selling his pictures would require a business license and a seller's permit. Beyond that, he would need a "green" card in order to work since he was a native of a foreign country.

Traversing the mountains would create a different set of problems for the old prospector. He would be competing with off road vehicles climbing over monstrous boulders and swift streams, disrupting his gold panning and certainly frightening his burros. During hunting season a bullet meant for a deer could find its way into Pete. Worse yet, he could be the victim of a violent crime while he wandered the highways and end up losing more than just his tools and shoes.

Pete was just an old man trying to make a living like everyone else. How he chose to do it was a little unconventional, even in the 1930s and 1940s. But that's what made him so unique and fascinating. When he and his burros came into town, people were there to greet them. He loved it. And he was ready to peddle his pictures, poems, and maybe a gold nugget.

Times and laws were different in 1936. California's eccentric old wanderer took a life while trying to protect his livelihood. This fact and the resulting trial made Pete infamous and a colorful part of California's history. His trial captured audiences far and wide and was dubbed "the trial of the decade."

Throughout the jubilation and celebrations that followed the trial, let's not forget that a family was left grieving and damned angry. Franklin Darcey left behind a wife and three young daughters. His widow was left with the painful job of telling her children about an eccentric old man who had killed their father and about an unjust verdict.

Did Pete accidentally shoot the attorney, or did he fire the shotgun intentionally during his rage? Certainly the townspeople took pity on the old guy. Did the jury also take pity on him? Was the judge sympathetic towards him? Could the prosecution have prepared a stronger case? Did pity enter into the prosecutor's mind? Since the transcript of the trial wasn't in the court's file, what happened to it?

Such was the judicial system in 1936. It certainly left more questions than answers. The truth about what really happened on that spring day in 1936 remains locked inside this worn, grimy pencil stub that I thoughtfully roll in my hands.

Although we are left wondering about a tragic incident, I turn the reader's attention to the old prospector's relationship with his burros. We can all learn from Pete and what his burros meant to him. We can learn about true friendship.

Pete made small fortunes over the years; however, he died without a dime in his pocket. Perhaps buried deep in California's Sierra Nevada Mountains lies some of that fortune, waiting to be found. Just like the black purse.

In conclusion, I wonder if indeed it was fate that brought me to write this story. Pete had ties to Auburn, California in the 1930s. My family ultimately moved to the Auburn area in 1958, and I attended high school there. My father's re-awakening of the old prospector's notoriety took place in an Auburn doctor's office, not far from what was once the Durfee's ranch. The story has truly come full circle.

Newspapers

Appeal-Democrat, May 1, 1933
San Francisco Chronicle, April 24, 1936
San Jose Mercury Herald, April – July 1936
Reno Evening Gazette, April 27, 1936
San Francisco Chronicle, July 4-8, 1936
Nevada State Journal, July 4, 1936
Auburn Journal, July 9, 1936
Syracuse (NY) Herald, August 12, 1936
Oakland Tribune, October 4, 1936
Oakland Tribune, December 11, 1936
Oakland Tribune, August 10, 1937
Nevada State Journal, October 24, 1937
Nevada State Journal, Sep 7, 1938
San Francisco Examiner, December 1938
Reno Evening Gazette, Jan 18, 1939
Oakland Tribune, August 6, 1946
Oakland Tribune, September 1946

Internet

Ancestry.com
Nma.org (Historical Gold Prices – 1833-Present)
Malakoff.com/goldcountry.jennylin
Webtech.kennesaw.edu (The Roaring Twenties)
Lib.umd.edu (San Francisco 1939-40)
Croatians.com (Neptune Fish Grotto)
Wikipedia.com (William I)

Court records, Santa Clara County Superior Court

About the Author

Brookelea Heintz Lutton grew up in the foothills of Northern California and has always had a keen interest in history. She has written a biography of her great grandfather August Jesse and continues to research and write her family's history. She has produced a Heritage Cookbook for family and friends. Her first published article, "Secrets," appeared in *Everton's Genealogical Helper* in 2008. She is a mother of two, grandmother of four, and lives in Elk Grove, California with her husband Ron and two beagles.